PRO GAMES
DINOSAURS
in THE BOY FROM THE CAVE

IN PREHISTORIC TIMES, MILLIONS OF YEARS AGO, DINOSAURS USED TO INHABIT THE EARTH. AMONG THE HUGE ANIMALS, THERE WAS A BABY CALLED DINGO. HE WAS VERY CURIOUS, AND THE LITTLE DINO BECAME A SUPER-ADVENTURER.

AF390954

ON A QUIET AFTERNOON, SOMETHING UNUSUAL HAPPENED: TWO METEORS CAME OUT OF SPACE AND FELL ON EARTH! ONE OF THEM FELL INTO A VOLCANO, AND THE OTHER ONE STOPPED AT A MORE DISTANT PLACE, CAUSING A BIG CRASH THAT SCARED THE DINOSAURS.
SPLOSH

WITH THE FALL OF THE METEOR,
THE VOLCANO ERUPTED, AND QUICKLY THE
LAVA BEGAN TO SPREAD. AT THE SAME TIME,
ALL THE DINOSAURS RAN FOR SHELTER.
FRIGHTENED AND NOT UNDERSTANDING WHAT
WAS HAPPENING, DINGO LOOKED FOR A
SHORTCUT TO GET TO HIS HOUSE.

AS HE WAS SCARED AND RUNNING AS FAST AS POSSIBLE, DINGO DIDN'T NOTICE THAT HE WAS STANDING ON TOP OF A CLIFF. WHEN HE REALIZED THAT, IT WAS ALREADY TOO LATE: HE COULDN'T STOP HIMSELF IN TIME AND FELL FROM THE TOP!

LUCKILY, DINGO FELL ON SOME TREES AND VINES, WHICH PREVENTED HIM FROM HURTING HIMSELF. HOWEVER, HE GOT CAUGHT IN THE VINES AND COULD NOT GET LOOSE AT ALL. ON TOP OF THAT, THERE WAS NO DINOSAUR NEAR THERE TO HELP HIM.

SUDDENLY, A MYSTERIOUS BEING APPEARED AMONG THE FOLIAGE OF THE TREE. HE WAS SMALL, CARRYING A CLUB IN HIS HAND AND WATCHING DINGO FROM A DISTANCE. JUST LIKE A PREDATOR, HE MADE NO NOISE OR SUDDEN MOVEMENTS, HE JUST STARED AT THE DINOSAUR.

WHEN DINGO LEAST EXPECTED IT, THE CREATURE SCREAMED AND JUMPED FROM THE TOP OF THE TREE, GOING TOWARDS HIM. AS HE WIELDED THE CLUB, DINGO THOUGHT HE WOULD SUFFER A TERRIBLE ATTACK.

AS HE FELT THE SMALL CREATURE COMING TOWARDS HIM IN FURY, DINGO CLOSED HIS EYES AND BEGAN TO TREMBLE WITH FEAR. HE EXPECTED TO RECEIVE A HEAVY HIT, BUT WAS SURPRISED TO REALIZE THAT THE MYSTERIOUS BEING HAD FREED HIM FROM THE BONDS OF THE VINE.
ZUM
PAK
PAK
PAK
PAK

DINGO FELL TO THE GROUND AND SLOWLY GOT UP. WHEN HE LOOKED FORWARD, HE SAW A CAVE BOY, WHO APPEARED ONLY TO RELEASE HIM FROM THE VINES. DINGO WAS AMAZED BY THE BOY'S INTELLIGENCE AND GENEROUS HEART.

THE TWO LOOKED AT EACH OTHER WITH FEAR AND, WITHOUT MAKING ANY THREATENING MOVEMENTS, APPROACHED EACH OTHER. AFTER REALIZING THAT THERE WAS NO DANGER, DINGO MADE A GESTURE OF GRATITUDE. THE BOY SMILED AND OPENED HIS ARMS TO THE DINOSAUR, WHO FOR THE FIRST TIME, RECEIVED A HUG. THERE, A BEAUTIFUL FRIENDSHIP WAS BORN!

THEY STARTED TO PLAY TOGETHER AND THE CAVE BOY GESTURED FOR DINGO TO FOLLOW HIM. HE WANTED TO SHOW THE DINOSAUR THE DRAWINGS HE HAD MADE ON THE WALLS OF HIS HOUSE.
POIM
POIM
POIM
13

WHEN THEY GOT INTO THE CAVE WHERE THE BOY
LIVED, DINGO FOUND IT WEIRD THAT THE BOY'S
PARENTS WERE NOT AT HIS HOUSE. BUT, WHEN HE
SAW THE DRAWINGS ON THE WALLS, THE DINOSAUR
NOTICED THAT HIS FRIEND'S FATHER HAD BEEN TAKEN
AS A SLAVE BY THE PTERODACTYLS OF THE SHADOWS.
HIS MOTHER, ON THE OTHER HAND, HAD GONE
OUT TO GET SOME FOOD.

WHEN HE LEFT THE CAVE, DINGO REMEMBERED THAT THERE WAS A VERY DARK PLACE WHERE HIS FRIEND'S FATHER MIGHT BE. HE THEN GESTURED FOR THE BOY TO FOLLOW HIM, AND TOGETHER THEY SET OFF ON A GREAT ADVENTURE.

ON THE WAY, DINGO AND HIS FRIEND SPOTTED THE METEOR THAT HAD FALLEN TO THE GROUND. AS IT CRACKLED AND HAD A STRONG GLOW, THE OBJECT CAUGHT BOTH OF THEIR ATTENTION. THEY APPROACHED THE LUMINOUS STONE WITH CURIOSITY.

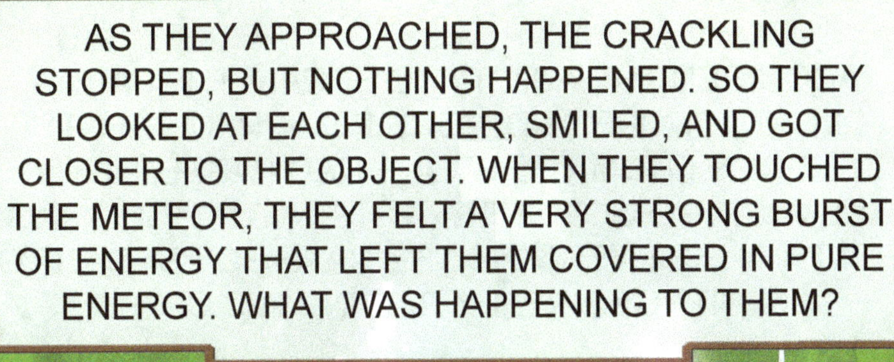

AS THEY APPROACHED, THE CRACKLING STOPPED, BUT NOTHING HAPPENED. SO THEY LOOKED AT EACH OTHER, SMILED, AND GOT CLOSER TO THE OBJECT. WHEN THEY TOUCHED THE METEOR, THEY FELT A VERY STRONG BURST OF ENERGY THAT LEFT THEM COVERED IN PURE ENERGY. WHAT WAS HAPPENING TO THEM?

SUDDENLY, THEY REALIZED THAT THEY HAD ACQUIRED THE ABILITY TO SPEAK. THEY ALSO FELT STRONGER AND MORE POWERFUL. ALL THE ENERGY FROM THE STONE HAD PASSED INTO THEM: DINGO GOT SUPER-STRENGTH LIGHTNING BOLTS IN HIS EYES, AND THE CAVE BOY BEGAN TO CONTROL FIRE BY RAISING HIS CLUB.

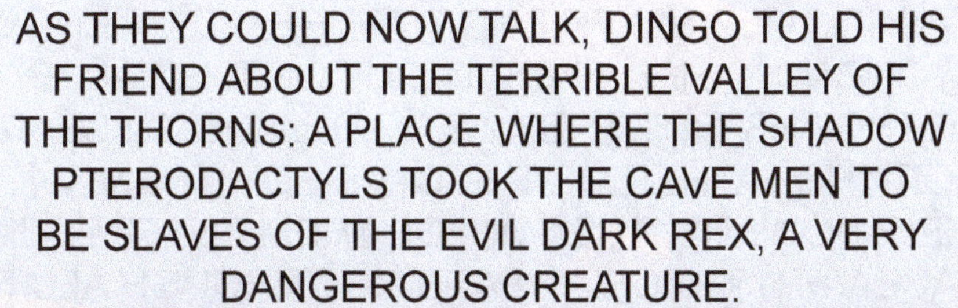

AS THEY COULD NOW TALK, DINGO TOLD HIS FRIEND ABOUT THE TERRIBLE VALLEY OF THE THORNS: A PLACE WHERE THE SHADOW PTERODACTYLS TOOK THE CAVE MEN TO BE SLAVES OF THE EVIL DARK REX, A VERY DANGEROUS CREATURE.

VALLEY OF THE THORNS

DINGO TOLD HIS FRIEND THAT HE DIDN'T KNOW ANYONE WHO HAD MADE IT OUT OF THE VALLEY OF THE THORNS, BUT THEY WERE WILLING TO SEARCH FOR THE FATHER OF THE CAVE BOY. THEN, WITH THEIR POWERS, THE TWO OF THEM ENTERED THE PLACE VERY QUICKLY, PASSING THROUGH ALL THE OBSTACLES AND DANGEROUS TRAPS.

POIM
POIM
POIM

WHEN THEY GOT CLOSE TO WHERE THE PRISONERS WERE, THE TWO STARTED TO BE ATTACKED BY THE PTERODACTYLS FROM THE SHADOWS. THEN, QUICKLY, THEY USED THEIR POWERS AND MANAGED TO SCARE THE ENEMIES FAR AWAY.
TUF
TUF
TUF

LOOKING AHEAD, THE BOY FOUND HIS FATHER TRAPPED IN ONE OF THE SLAVE'S CAGES. BEFORE HE COULD FREE HIM, THE DARK REX APPEARED AND JUMPED IN FRONT OF THE BOY AND DINGO, SHOWING HIS MONSTROUS STRENGTH. WITH HIS THREATENING RED EYES, HE TRIED TO INTIMIDATE THEM.

THE TWO WERE NOT AFRAID AND WENT INTO A FIERCE FIGHT WITH THE VILLAIN, WHO PROVED TO BE WILLING TO DO ANYTHING TO WIN THE BATTLE. THERE WAS A LOT OF JUMPING, HITTING, AND RUNNING, BUT THE DARK REX DID NOT GIVE UP TRYING TO TRAP THE TWO LITTLE WARRIORS.

AFTER THE LONG BATTLE, DINGO AND THE CAVE BOY DECIDED TO UNITE THEIR POWERS. THEN, WITH A BURST OF ENERGY AND FIRE, THEY STRUCK AND KNOCKED THE DARK REX INTO THE MISSING LINK HOLE. AT LAST, THEY MANAGED TO FREE THE SLAVES FROM THE EVIL DINOSAUR.
PERIGO

IMMEDIATELY, THE CAVE BOY RAN TOWARDS HIS FATHER, WHO HUGGED HIS SON. HE AND ALL THE OTHER SLAVES WERE VERY HAPPY TO BE FREE AND TO HAVE TWO STRONG HEROES TO FIGHT THE EVIL DINOSAURS. THANKS TO THE TWO FRIENDS, NO ONE ELSE WOULD HAVE TO BE AFRAID TO WALK THROUGH THE WORLD OF DINOSAURS AGAIN.

DINGO AND HIS FRIEND WERE VERY HAPPY, FOR NOT ONLY HAD THE CAVE BOY'S FATHER RETURNED HOME, BUT THEY WERE BOTH GETTING STRONGER AND MORE POWERFUL. BUT, JUST WHEN THEY THOUGHT ALL WAS QUIET, THEY RECEIVED NEWS THAT AN INNOCENT DINOSAUR HAD BEEN LOST IN THE ICE VALLEY. WASTING NO TIME, THE BOY DRESSED IN HIS COMBAT CLOTHES, RAISED HIS CLUB, CLIMBED ONTO DINGO'S BACK AND, LOUDLY, SAID: "MY NAME IS KIMBO. ME AND MY FRIEND DINGO ARE GOING TO SAVE ALL NATIONS AND BRING THEM JOY. THE POWER IS IN OUR HANDS! LET'S GO!"
FIM